George Ambrose Dennison

Songs and Lyrics

George Ambrose Dennison

Songs and Lyrics

ISBN/EAN: 9783744652346

Printed in Europe, USA, Canada, Australia, Japan

Cover: Foto ©Thomas Meinert / pixelio.de

More available books at **www.hansebooks.com**

SONGS AND LYRICS

BY

GEORGE AMBROSE DENNISON

G. P. PUTNAM'S SONS

NEW YORK: 27 & 29 WEST 23D STREET
LONDON: 25 HENRIETTA STREET, COVENT GARDEN

1884

Press of
G. P. Putnam's Sons
New York

TO

MY FRIEND

R. W. W.

CONTENTS.

		PAGE
INVOCATION	. . . .	vii
TO A BLUEBELL	. . . .	1
ON THE HEIGHTS	. . . .	3
TO A CRICKET	. . . . . .	4
A MESSENGER	. . . .	6
SORROW	. . . .	8
FAREWELL	. . . .	11
BREEZES	. . . .	15
SONNET	. . . .	17
MY LOVE IS LIKE A FLAME	. . . .	18
A NIGHT SONG	. . . .	19
DIVINE COMPASSION	. . . . . .	20
SONG	. . . .	22
BE PATIENT, HEART	. . . . . .	23
WOOING IN VAIN	. . . . . .	25
A SUMMONS	. . . .	26
AN OFFERING	. , ...	32
HOPE	. . . .	33
A NIGHT RIDE	. . . .	34
TO THE POET	. . . .	38
TO MY MUSE	. . . .	39

CONTENTS.

	PAGE
To the Wood Thrush	43
At Dawn	46
The Forest Stream	49
Mine	53
To a Dying Friend	56
Beyond Words	58
Spring	60
Nightfall from the Mountain	65
An Invitation	69
Spring Night	73
The Pine Tree	74
Transformation	79
A Vision of Poesy	80
The Muse Disdainful	84
To the Sea	88

INVOCATION.

Lead me, O Muse, by waters clear and sweet,

Where tones of liquid harmony arise,

Where forms of woodland beauty charm my eyes,

And changing light and shade my glances meet ;

Lead where my gaze the laughing Dawn may greet,

Or where the golden glory of the skies

On Evening's dusky bosom slowly dies,

And stately Night walks forth with dewy feet.

Thus guided, I may shun those turgid springs

Whose waters creep through dark and devious ways,

And taste the well of undefiled delight ;

And hearkening unto Nature while she sings,

My voice at last a worthy song may raise,

As free as air, and clear as morning light.

TO A BLUEBELL.

Modest bell,
  Sunny bank adorning,
Passing well
  Thou dost grace the morning.
Winds caress thee as they go,
Swing thee gently to and fro,
Kiss, and kiss, they love thee so,
  Other blossoms scorning.

They would fain
  Cease their idle playing,
And remain,
  Never from thee straying ;
For with lovely playfulness
Thou returnest each caress,

I

Or dost bow in humbleness,
    Like a spirit praying.

If my verse,
    In some woodland measure,
Might rehearse
    All thy beauty's treasure,
Strains so fresh and pure should rise,
Every heart beneath the skies
Would awake in glad surprise
    To a new-born pleasure.

Yet, my bell,
    Though I sang forever,
Ne'er so well,
    With my best endeavor,
That illusive charm of thine,
Finer far than word or sign,
Nameless, rare, almost divine—
    I could sing it never.

ON THE HEIGHTS.

Below us, smiling at her best,
   In royal summer's rich array,
The glad earth wears such happy face
   As rounds with joy a perfect day.

O'er yonder hills and yonder stream
   The eye delighted wanders wide,
Yet gladly do I turn and gaze
   On finer beauty at my side.

For though that broad expanse may show
   The fairest scene beneath the skies,
All that, and more, looks out on me
   From these two worlds, my Lady's eyes.

TO A CRICKET

SINGING AT NIGHT ON BROADWAY.

———

Thou jocund songster, what has brought thee here
   To this abode of haggard toil and care?
Why dost thou chirrup forth thy sprightly cheer
   Upon this foul and inattentive air?

The joy of living soundeth in thy voice—
   A simple verity, a happy call
On all that hear thy summons, to rejoice
   That life is sweet, and ill can ne'er befall.

The home for thee were surely far away,
   Beside a hearth in some sequestered place,
Where worthy labor glorifies the day,
   And sweet contentment shines in every face.

4

Thy song would there a happy circle greet,

And every note of thine would harmonize

With hours that run forever pure and sweet,—

With peace that soothes, and joy that never dies.

The song of birds that hail the morning light,

The drone of locusts to the drowsy noon,

The voice of winds that usher in the night,

Would all accord with thy melodious tune.

But simple gladness and the joy of song

Are sadly alien to this busy place,

Where servile slaves of Mammon daily throng,

And rude contention rules the dizzy race.

And yet methinks thou seemest well content

To chirrup thus, where'er thy lot may be:

Though in a dungeon close thy life were spent,

Thy simple song would make a world for thee.

A MESSENGER.

Wind, you never have blown so sweet
    As you blow to-day ;
Never before could your voice repeat
    Half so rich a lay ;
For you come from where my lady dwells,
And the burden of your music tells
    What a rapture lights her eye,
    What a fragrance fills her sigh,
What a tender grace
Plays upon her spirit-quickened face.

Return, O Wind, and tell
The maid I love so well,
    That the day is long without her,
    Night is racked with dreams about her,

A MESSENGER.

And my breast

Can know not rest

Till my eyes again behold her,—

Till my arms once more enfold her.

SORROW.

Sorrow came one day and said to me,
" I would dwell for evermore with thee."
  But I liked her not, and cried, "Away!"
  For she cast a gloom upon the day,
And a chill was in her breath,
And her eye foreshadowed death.
  But my rude rebuffs were vain,
  For she answered me again,
Saying: " Nay, do not deny me,
Do not seek to fly me.
  That unthinking boy,
  Rosy-featured Joy,
Whose vain windings thou dost follow,
Hath a heart both false and hollow.
  Let him go, and take thou me

In his stead, and I will be

Always faithful unto thee."

Thus she spoke, and calming my alarms,

Drew me to her with her saintly arms;

And she sang in measures soft and slow,

Sadly sweet and low,

Something Joy had never spoken,

Something heavenly, as a token

Of a perfect peace and rest

Waiting for me, in her breast.

Such persuasive sweetness had her song,

That my heart went out to her ere long;

And my wayward soul was won

To paths of peace, where quiet waters run.

And now sweet Sorrow dwells with me,

Evermore my friend to be.

Restlessness and change are flown,

Joy's distempers are unknown.

Under skies of placid gray
Quietly I sit all day,
  While from off the sea of Peace
  Zephyrs blow, and never cease.
Death, whose very name was once a fear,
On his journeys often passes near.
  Beautifully gentle is his face,
  Shining bright, as with an inward grace ;
And he seems a friend to Sorrow,
For they smile, and give " Good-morrow."
  Oft he speaks with me,
  And I dimly see
Other lands, I know not where,
Happy, and forever fair,
  Unto whose bright realms, some day
  He will spirit me away.
Not till dawns that happy morrow
Will I say good-bye to gentle Sorrow.

FAREWELL.

Come nearer, O beloved ! for my day
Is passing, and a radiance from beyond
Steals through the waning barrier that divides,
And grows, and grows, as that dissolves forever.
From out the shadows stretches forth a hand
And beckons me.   Nay, weep not, weep not so ;
For in that kindly palm no terror lies,
But perfect rest and everlasting peace.

Draw me close—closer, dear.   A faintness steals
Upon me, and my spirit fails—and fails.

   *   *   *   *   *   *   *   *

Have I been dreaming ?   I was there again,
Strolling along the border of that wood
Where happiness first found me, years ago.

How beautiful the day was !   All the air

Was fragrant with the balmy breath of May.

And you were there, Eugenia ; and you stood,

A vision of delight, with face upraised,

Watching the oriole building in the elm.

You held a spray of blossoms in your hand,

And watching still, as, rapt in what you saw,

You raised the flowers and pressed them to your

    face.

What was it in the movement of your arm,

Ere yet I saw your face, that thrilled me so,

And made me stop and gaze, scarce knowing why?

And then—how I remember !—as I passed,

The momentary, sweet entanglement

Of glances, and the flush that lit your face,

And then the sudden falling of your eyes :

How wonderful it was !   I paused, as though

A cord stretched out and held me to the spot ;

And then I went my way.

All things were changed.

The trees, the flowers, the grass, the very weeds

Had voices ; and they chanted to my heart

A ravishment of intermingling songs.

How wide the fields were grown ! How high the

trees !

And yonder stream, how beautiful it shone

With forms of wedded clouds and azure sky,

Made glorious by that bright, new-risen sun.

I wondered at the tumult in my breast,

Unknowing that in one brief space our hearts—

Our spirits—met, as now, alas, they part.

I saw it all, Eugenia, in the dream.

The world since then has been a paradise ;

For I have viewed it through your better eyes,

And from your finer spirit always shone

A light that radiated every where,

And wrapped the earth in glory.

               Oh ! again

That hand—that gracious, comfort-bearing hand !

How close it comes now—and that heavenly light—

    *   *   *   *   *   *   *   *

Alas, I wander.—Closer—closer dear,

And press my head upon that gentle breast,

So I may hear the heart-throbs, and may chain

My truant sense to them, and it shall stray

No more from you.   For now the change is near ;

And, till the last faint flutter of my breath,

My sight must still be true, that it may drink

The holy soul-light shining through your eyes—

The hand comes nearer—nearer—see ! the flame—

I lose you, O Eugenia—wife—farewell !

BREEZES.

Gentle breezes,

Joyful breezes,

Whither go ?

Daily, nightly,

Flitting lightly

To and fro.

Ever coming, ever going,

Undulating touch bestowing—

Strains that set my heart a-going,

Gentle breezes,

Whither go ?

Tuneful breezes,

Whisp'ring breezes,

O, how sweet !

What a blessing

15

Such caressing

Breath to meet !

Filled with tales of flower and tree,

Warbling bird and wandering bee,

Rush of stream and roar of sea,—

Tuneful breezes,

O, how sweet !

Loving breezes,

Heavenly breezes,—

Ah, divine !

All the essence

Of your presence

Make it mine.

With your grace my heart endow,

Keep it always sweet as now,—

To your purity I bow,

Loving breezes,

Ah, divine !

SONNET.

Like some great tear transformed to liquid gold,
  The evening star hangs tremulously clear,
  And near it lines of crimson cloud appear,
Whose beauty makes the heart leap to behold ;
Reflected, and repeated many fold,
  Upon the gentle river flowing near,
  To loving eyes a beauty shines, more dear
Than star and cloud in their own place can hold.
For lo ! the glories of the waning west
  Are wrought to lovelier issue by the play
Of wavering lights, and ceaseless interflow
Of form and color on the river's breast,
  Where Mystery seems her heavenly hand to lay,
And somewhat of diviner grace bestow.

MY LOVE IS LIKE A FLAME.

My love is like a flame that circles me,
  And I the dusky centre in that flame :
Changed by its light, all things on land and sea
  Wear a new beauty, bear a sweeter name.

O blesséd flame ! O pure, transforming light !
  When thou art summoned death's eclipse to
    bear,
Thy shadowy centre will dissolve in night,
  And die of its own darkness and despair !

A NIGHT SONG.

Upon the vast mid-silence of the night,
  A forest-bird awakens into song ;
So sweet he sings, and with such joyous might,
  The dark wood rings with music loud and long.

Alas, deluded songster ! yonder light
  Thou hailest thus is not the coming day ;
'T is but the pallid moon deceives thy sight,
  And with false promise steals thy song away.

Yet, not in vain hast thou with woodland art
  Moved unto melody the midnight air ;
For thou hast eased my overburdened heart,
  And long thy heavenly chant will linger there.

DIVINE COMPASSION.

Weary with the unavailing struggle
After light, when days were naught but darkness,
Utterly cast down beneath the burden
Of appalling doubt, and dread foreboding,
Whose despair heaped mountains on my spirit,
Crushing faith, and stifling high endeavor—
Tired of these, and longing for deliverance,
"Come, soul-winging Death," I cried, "and bear me
From this prison-house, where Mystery holds us
In a mesh no hand of man may sever."

Winds of night, that roused the gentle valley
Rudely from repose, and o'er the forest
Poured a song of noisy lamentation,
Sank at last upon the breast of Silence.

Black and angry was the face of heaven

With the host of clouds that stormed across it,

Shutting out the eyes of night, and shedding

Deathly gloom on all that lay beneath them.

But behind the fury-driven vapors

Waited peace ; for soon the clouds departed,

And behold !—the shadow-smile of heaven.

From the silent chambers of the midnight

Came a message of divine compassion.

Voiceless to the ear, its tones were vibrant,

Full of hope and vivifying gladness

To my heavy, grief-enshrouded spirit.

Winds arose again, but now melodious,

Bearing on their wings a song of triumph.

And again the voices of the forest

Swelled, but chanted peace. Despair was van-
    quished

In the light of hope, that beamed effulgent

With the glory of a joy eternal.

SONG.

The winds will come, the winds will go,
The buds will burst, the flowers will blow,
The seas will always ebb and flow,
   And naught remain the same.

The love I bear thee fares not so ;
'T will never fail, 't will never go,
But, steadfast more than words cán show,
   'T will burn, a deathless flame.

BE PATIENT, HEART.

A voice, a something in me wakes
    And sings sweet music all day long,
As some close hidden warbler makes ·
    The vale melodious with his song.

Yet, often as my weak hand tries
    To give the yearning child a tongue,
I hear but inarticulate cries,
    The message still remains unsung.

Be patient, heart, await the word ;
    Thy haste subdue, thy strings attune
To songs of wind, and stream, and bird,
    And all the notes of this glad June.

Dwell in the woods, and let them play
　　Upon thee, thrill thee through and through ;
Bathe in the golden light of day,
　　And drink the pearls of evening dew.

When they have wrought within thee so
　　That thou art one with all things fair,
When in thy soil the roses grow
　　And through thy chamber breathes the air,

Then thou shalt sing as free as they,
　　As sweet as theirs thy song shall rise ;
The bars that hold shall fall away,
　　Thy song mount upward to the skies.

WOOING IN VAIN.

Though I woo her,
  The Goddess scorns to sing;
Though I sue her,
  She never moves a wing,
But holds herself aloof,
Nor cares for my behoof.

  I will woo no more, but wait;
  For her coldness will abate
By and by, and she will come, and rest
In the deepest chamber of my breast.

  If too long I plead,
  Though at length she heed,
I may find her, not a heavenly maid,
But a sorry, inharmonious jade,
  With eye that sees obscurely,
  With voice that sings not purely,
With coarse and vulgar face,
Devoid of all that breathes poetic grace.

25

A SUMMONS.

Weary toiler, come away !
Woods are green, fields are gay,
    Everywhere the winds are playing,
    Over rocky summits straying,
Over meadows, where the grass
Bows to gentle breaths that pass,
    Where divinely fragrant flowers are blowing,
    Where the vernal tide of life is flowing.

Every living thing
Celebrates the spring
    With a song,
    While along
By the banks of running streams,
Voices whisper sweet as dreams.

Overhead, the trees

Rustle in the breeze,

Hearing many a secret tale

Brought from far-off hill and dale,—

Tales of woodland bowers

Filled with fragrant flowers ;

Tales of happy things that skip and run,—

Sparkling waters laughing in the sun.

Come forth, O friend ! come forth, and see

How heavenly fair the world can be ;

Come with me, and you shall rest

On the mountain's rugged breast ;

Come, and learn the peace of balmy vales,

Breathe the perfume of the flying gales.

Zephyrs there will meet you,

All things fair will greet you,

Nature's songs will harmonize

Your weary heart with bending skies,

And every joyous thing

Will wake your heart to sing.

Beneath those skies

Grand pæans rise

Out of the valley of peace,

Flying abroad, till they cease

Their glad, melodious flight

In the hush of the rapturous night.

Come away, poor, burrowing mole !

Leave this prison of the soul

Where you waste the hours

And misuse your powers.

You shall rest your weary eyes

On a host of clouds that rise

From waters rolling far away,

Beyond the outer realms of day.

In forms of snowy white,

In fields of heavenly light,

From the farthest western lands

To the eastern sea-girt sands,

High above in splendid masses,

All day long the legion passes.

If they shine too dazzling bright

On your unaccustomed sight,

Turn your toil-worn eyes away

To those restful forms of gray

That like a field Elysian lie

Above the mountains in the southern sky.

Come, and hear the joyful notes

From a thousand feathered throats.

Such a beauty all around is springing,

Such a sweetness every breeze is bringing,

Through the forest shades,

Through the sunny glades,

And the winding streams along,

That joy runs over into song.

Down the great ledges of stone

Rushes the brook, with a tone

    So utterly clear

    And sweet to the ear,

    It will make your heart happy to hear.

Winds will woo you

And renew you,

Rouse your spirit, and endue you

    With the pulse of springing life

    That through all of nature's forms is rife.

If your heart is sore opprest,

If you long for perfect rest,

    You shall wander where

    Scarce a breath of air

Stirs the leafy walls

Of dim woodland halls.

    Never song of jubilant bird

    In that placid vale is heard,

But calmly, from remotest depths, the dove
Breathes forth the simple story of his love.
 Mortal voice nor footfall ever sounds
 In the precincts of those hallowed grounds :
No rude presence breaks the perfect calm
That abides there, like a heavenly balm.

A glory lies on every hand,
Over realms of sea and land.
 Come then, toiler, ere it be too late ;
 Nature calls you, but she will not wait.
Come from darkness unto day ;
Nay, tarry not, but come, O come away !

AN OFFERING.

No gift of precious gems I bear,
  Nor gold, nor aught that wealth commands,
But things that prove themselves more rare—
  A loyal heart, and willing hands.

Relentless Time, whose hard decrees
  Condemn all riches to decay,
Shall purify and strengthen these,
  To serve you till your latest day.

HOPE.

Through the depth of my soul's dark cloud,

Through my spirit's enveloping shroud,

    A great light came,

    As the light of a conquering flame.

And the sound of a voice I heard,

As the song of a carolling bird,

    Whose heaven-sent lay

    Drove the compassing vapors away.

And the path of my future was sweet

With flowers that invited my feet,

    And skies grew clear,

    And glowed with a smile of good cheer.

And over an orient sea

A white hand beckoned to me,

    Till my storm-beat soul

    Saw the light of its ultimate goal.

A NIGHT RIDE.

'T is a gallop of hungering fire,

For my heart is ablaze with desire !

   Through his sinewy frame

   Yorick thrills to the flame

Of my love, and he never can tire.

His shoulders are massive and strong,

His stride is elastic and long,

   And the rhythmical beat

   Of his musical feet

Is sweet as the swing of a song.

He exults in the speed of the race,

In the spring and the stretch of his pace ;

   For our swift course lies

Toward the light of her eyes—

Toward the wonderful light of her face.

Away ! my good lad, to the strand ;

Away ! to the edge of the land.

   When the gallop is o'er

   And you stand at her door,

You shall feel the caress of her hand.

Though fleet as an arrow he flies,

Though sundering space swiftly dies,

   My heart cries " Oh, haste !

   All time is a waste

Till I drink of her soul at her eyes ! "

Far down the dark land, where the lea

Is caressed by the lip of the sea,

   Pure and sweet as the May,

   Fresh and bright as the day,

A maiden holds night-watch for me.

My heart is athrob with delight ;

For there, in the depth of the night,

Like a soul-guiding star

In the heavens afar,

I catch the faint gleam of her light.

Ho ! for the beacon that gleams !

For the light of her passion that streams !

The fire in my heart

Like a flame-feathered dart,

Leaps forth and unites with its beams.

The gloomy pine-forest is past,

The sea-meadow opens at last ;

Now away to her door

By the billowy shore,

Like a home-winging bird on the blast !

Oh ! listen, love ; listen and hear

The hurrying hoofs coming near.

Let the eloquent air,

As it tosses your hair,

Sing the sounds of approach to your ear.

At last ! draw rein—it is o'er !

Yet, Yorick, one mighty leap more !

O'er the gate at a bound—

Up the lane—to the ground—

A shadowy form at the door.

TO THE POET.

Buried in the shadows of the forest,

The wood-bird pours his notes.

Where the mountain heavenward rears its summit,

The wind-voice breathes its song.

Though no mortal hears they care not,

Heeding nought beyond the songs they sing.

O my Poet, though the world contemn thee,

And pass thee by unheard,

Though the loftiest breathings of thy spirit

Awake no answering tone,

Be thou faithful to the power within thee,

Be thou ever happy in thy song.

TO MY MUSE.

Fly, my Muse, with all fair things that be,
And bring the spirit of beauty back to me.

Follow the stream, my Muse ;
Listen, and bring me news
　　Of the shadow-haunted fell,
　　Of the blossom-scented dell,
Of the limpid mother-fountain,
High upon the rugged mountain.

Listen close, and hear it sing
How the hours forever bring
　　Mists that creep, and dews that fall,
　　Rains that bring new life to all.
How the mountain to his breast
Draws them, holds them there at rest

Till they seem a part

Of his very heart ;

How he gives them forth again,

Sends them singing to the main,

Saying, " Ye are part of me ;

Go, and mingle with the sea."

Mount, and meet the clouds on high,

Whose glory of color emblazons the sky ;

Rise where the topmost crest

Answers the darkening West

With a farewell glow,

While, sleeping below

In the arms of encompassing night,

Earth glimmers, and fades on the sight.

Mount to the cirri, that play

With winds that bear them away ;

That flare like flames, and curl,

As through the rare ether they whirl

In a swift, mad race

To be first, when the face

Of dawn peeps over the edge of the sea,—

To blush with her ravishing kisses, and flee

On, on to day's hot fire,

And melt in the bliss of attained desire.

Away, my muse ! away !

Into the west with the day !

Speed with thy might,

Fly with the night,

Fly with the shadowy hours of delight !

Hasten, nor brook delay !

Away !   Away !

Flow with the waters free,

Journey afar with the sea.

Leap with the dash and the roar,

Mingle with breakers that buffet the shore.

Whither the storm may flee,

Follow the sea.

Float, float, at rest,

Float on ocean's breast ;

 Where the glassy waters lie

 Tranquil as the bending sky.

Still, still, beneath the noonday light,

Still, still, beneath the dome of night.

 On the long, majestic swell

 Sleep, sleep, and learn the spell

Of the waters rising, falling,

Spirit-soothing, sense-enthralling.

Fly, my muse, with all fair things that be,

And bring the spirit of beauty back to me.

TO THE WOOD THRUSH.

O bright brown bird ! O master-bird of song !

Your music thrills and melts me to a mood

Of breathless ecstasy !   From out the grove

Of lofty trees, whose unincumbered trunks

Raise toward the sky their canopy of leaves,

You fill the soul of morning with delight.

Some tones in common other songsters sing,

But yours are yours alone.   That higher gladness,

That tone of calm aloofness in the strains,

Is never heard from other throat than yours.

The song is minor, yet is never sad ;

It seems the voice of a tender spirit, poised

In saintly contemplation of sweet things.

Methinks you care not for variety ;

But having listened well to nature's sounds—

To bird notes, and the notes of singing streams—

The ever-changing harmonies of the wind—

The eager hope that fills the song of Morn—

The larger music of consoling Night—

You blend the very soul of every tone,

And pour it forth in this clear, woodland song.

In vain I try to find some word, or phrase,

Or symbol, that shall show the quality

That gives the charm, and makes your song su-
      preme.

Yours only is the master power to move

My inner sense with intervals as sweet,

As full of joy, as those at heaven's gate

That yester-night I wept to in my dreams.

Some metal, finer than the world has known,

If rightly shaped, and blown upon by winds

That move it to vibration, might give forth

Such perfect tones as these.   But never, sure,

Can thought attain to such sweet bliss of sound

As holds me while you pour upon my ear

The rapture of those round, slow, trill-like tones.

Sing on, my Silver-throat ! I lie among

The flowers, that listen with me, and I hear

A voice arisen from the golden days

Long past, when men were well content to sit

And listen in sweet leisure to the sounds

Of Nature, mother-singer of the world.

Moved by the classic beauty of your song

My soul floats backward to that distant time,

And hears fresh music in the running stream,—

A tone of new-born gladness in the wind.

AT DAWN.

Awake, my lady fair !

Dawn is in the air !

  In the eastern portals low

    Morning spreads her ruddy glow.

From the lusty robin's throat

Songs of salutation float

    Over the meadow wide,

    By the river's side,

Where the nodding buttercup

Holds its golden saucer up

    With a welcome gay

    To the growing day.

The world is at her freshest now ;

Come and see, my dearest, how

Everything seems to spring

With the life the sunbeams bring.

Haste ! O haste !

Come and taste

This bounding joy

Without alloy ;

For when the sun mounts high,

The sweetest part will die.

Streams are singing,

Birds are flinging

All around

Pearls of sound,

From the trees, the twigs, the ground.

Beads of dew

Wait for you,

Hold the thirsty sun at bay

Till your feet shall pass their way.

Things the sweetest, things the rarest,

Wait to welcome you, my fairest ;

But the fondest greeting lies

Here, belovéd, in my eyes.

    Lady mine, come forth and see ;

Come, O come to me !

THE FOREST STREAM.

Far in the depth of the forest

Wanders the fairest of waters.

Songs of the woodland it murmurs,

Caught from the wind in the branches,

From the deep chant of the pine tree,

From the light voice of the maple.

Songs of melodious warblers,

Cries of swift birds in their passage,

Flying above in the darkness

Unto the great Sleeping Water.

Calls of the conquering eagle,

Vanishing notes of the wood-dove,

Love-tones of shy, furry creatures—

All are absorbed and commingled

In the sweet song of the water.

Branches bend down from above it,

Sweep it with gentle caresses.

On the great boulders, the mosses

Gleam with an emerald brightness,

Shine with the spray drops they gather

Where the stream tosses and tumbles.

Happy the days when I follow

Gentle and sweet Singing Water,

Led as a child by the streamlet,

Through the dim aisles of the forest.

O! the rare beauty it gathers

Unto itself, as it dances

Through the great heart of the woodland!

Softly it gurgles and murmurs

Out of its innermost currents,

Singing the wonderful secrets

Learned in the bosom of nature.

Where the stream pauses and widens

Into a pool, with the margin

Rising abruptly above it,

Guarded in silent seclusion

By the great trees, with their branches

Spreading and crossing in shadow,

There do I oftentimes linger,

Gazing down into the water.

In the clear depths I discover

Borders of grasses and blossoms,

Masses of sheltering verdure,

And, perchance, gleaming below them,

Far below branches and tree tops,

Greets me the azure of heaven.

.

Happy, O child of the forest,

Happy your life in the wildwood.

Nature, your brown-breasted mother,

Lovingly close to her bosom

Holds you, and while the deep midnight

Filters its starlight upon you,

While the bright blaze of the noontide

Lightens your face through the shadows,

Closer she holds you, and softly

Whispers unknowable secrets.

MINE.

I know a stream of pure delight, that flows
Through quiet ways, and everywhere it goes,
  Joy dances after
  With song and laughter.
Sweet purity defends it,
Love every beauty lends it,
  And from its source,
  Throughout its course,
The fairest grace attends it.

Not alone to eyes of mine
Does this queen of waters shine.
  Many a one that loves it, knows
  How serenely sweet it flows,
From mysterious regions bringing

Beauties rare, and sweetly singing

   Strains that wake the heart to gladness,

   Raise it to a gentle madness,

Under whose transforming power

New delights illumine every hour.

But to me, to me alone,

Is that finer beauty shown

   That beneath the surface lies,

   Hidden from all other eyes.

Grace and sweetness meet my gaze

In those depths, and lo ! the rays

   Of an inner light I see,

   Many-hued, that shines alone for me.

And the under-currents sing

Melodies that ring, and ring

   Through my heart of hearts in perfect harmony.

Deep I gaze, and there

I see my face, so fair

That scarce I know it ;

For the waters show it

Freed of every line that mars.

And a light as pure as light of stars,

Tender as the blue of skies,

Beams upon me from the eyes.

And my thoughts are rendered back to me

By that face of purity,

Lucent as the light of day,

With all the dark and gross refined away.

Sing out ! Sing out for joy, my heart !

The stream is mine, and never will we part.

TO A DYING FRIEND.

Methought I stood upon a lofty hill,

And saw, above the dim horizon line,

Lighting the westward portals of the South,

The slender moon.   So passing fair it shone—

So like a thing of heaven—that to gaze

Upon its face with my unhallowed eyes

Seemed profanation.   Slowly came a cloud

From the remotest chambers of the sky.

Sombre as night it was ; of hideous shape,

Like some devouring monster.   On it crept,

With slow, resistless pace, until its long,

Gaunt, forward-reaching arms embraced the moon,

That seemed to shrink away in helpless fright.

Then came the creature's body ; and the orb

Was swallowed up within it, and devoured.

I turned away in horror at the sight,

And wept that aught so pure and beautiful

Should suffer black destruction. Then, methought,

While evening winds went wailing, and all things

Seemed weeping with me at the sad eclipse,

From out the air above a gentle voice,

In sweetest tones, spake solace to me thus :

" Be comforted.   The orb whose loss you mourn

Is not a waning, but a crescent moon ;

And though 't is hidden from your vision now,

Another night will see it shine aloft

In full-orbed majesty.   Such glorious light,

Such amplitude of beauty, will it show,

That all the earth will gladden at the sight."

Thus reassured, I turned again ; and lo !

Where I had seen a monster in the sky,

With truer sight I now beheld a shape

Whose face was calm, beneficent, and sweet.

BEYOND WORDS.

In vain—in vain—I cannot tell thee, Sweet,
  How more than life I love thee ;
My tongue as well might number all the sands,
  Or name the stars above me.

Not though I chose the choicest words e'er penned
  In praise of Love's best treasure,
And coined one perfect, soul-entrancing phrase,
  In Love's divinest measure.

But think how yonder pallid maid, the moon,
  Is worshipped by the ocean,
Whose pulses through the ages rise and fall
  In measureless devotion.

58

Think how that mighty lover evermore
  His million voices raises
Throughout his vast dominions round the world,
  To chant his lady's praises.

High as the moon above the ocean reigns,
  So high thou art above me ;
With passion far outreaching ocean's realms,
  Eternally I love thee !

SPRING.

When the Maiden came, her presence,
Like a rare, ethereal essence,
    Scarce was known, she stole so shy,
    Shrinking from the bitter sky,
Stepping tip-toe here and there
With a foot as light as air.
    On the hills, a tender flush,
    A rosy-purple blush,
Showed the spirit rife
Of the newly wakened life.

They that love her well
Felt the mystic spell,
    Felt their blood rush full and free,
    As the sap runs in the tree.

Signs they found where shooting branches grow,

By streams whose liberated waters flow ;

   Where, between the morn and night,

   The willow buds all burst in white.

They read the welcome news

In the tender hues

   Of many a verdant spray,

   That lustier throve with every fostering day.

Many a time hath she been here,

Many a time hath fled in fear ;

   For old Winter, loth to yield his place,

   Met her joyance with a frowning face ;

And from his icy mouth

He blew upon the South

   A sudden breath

   Of chilly death.

But all his stormy buffetings were vain,

For though he smote her, yet she came again ;

   And ever she came stronger,

And ever she stayed longer.

　　Half she fought him, half she wooed him,

　　Half she bade, and half she sued him,

Growing gentler day by day

As his fury passed away.

　　Each groping root,

　　Each springing shoot,

Every leaf that met the sight,

Every vine that sought the light,

　　And streams that gurgled all

　　Because the icy thrall

Was melting fast

And could not last,—

　　Here, and there, and everywhere,

　　Brought resistless power to bear

On the Maiden's foe,

Till his valor melted low.

Then with willing vines she bound him,

Threw her rosy arms around him,

Charmed him with her violet eyes,

Soothed his anger, hushed his sighs,

Held him, drew him to her breast,

Lapped him in forgetful rest.

   And the Maiden sang,

   And the music rang

In the dying Monarch's ears

As the music of the spheres.

   She sang so sweet, she sang so long,

   She overcame him with her song.

Into hers she drew his breath,

And lured him, calm and powerless, unto Death.

And now, O happy day !

The Maiden 's here to stay.

She, the wonder-singer,

She, the sweet joy bringer ;

   Spirit, potent everywhere,

   In the waters, in the air,

Leaping with the pulsing light,

Resting in the silent soul of night.

   Would you view her from afar ?

   She is in the morning star ;

Would you have her near?

She awaits you here

   In every thing that grows,

   In every happy stream that flows.

Do but hear how divinely she sings !

Do but see the rare beauty she brings !

   Hear the music of caroling birds ;

   Hear the lowing and bleating of herds;

Hear the long, low sigh of the pines

By the pool, where the night star shines.

   Her banner of hope is unfurled,

   Her mantle envelops the world.

Buried beauty receives a new birth,

The spirit of joy is abroad on the earth.

NIGHTFALL FROM THE MOUNTAIN.

The last beam fades, the peace of evening falls,
Upon the broad domain of dying day
Broods saintly Silence, save that, faint and sweet,
The sound of evening bells in shadowed vales
Floats, a sweet chant of rest, o'er all the land.
It steals along the placid lakes and streams,
Up the vast reaches of the mountain side,
Lingers a moment on this height, and wakes
A sense of rapture in the listening ear
Ere soaring skyward from this baser mould,
To join the harmonies at heaven's gate.

Rising from out the wooded gulf that yawns
A measureless depth below, the fragrant breath

Of forests never trod by foot of man,

Like nature's balmy benediction, floats

Upon the pulseless bosom of the air.

Sweet is the breath as airs from flowery isles

Exhaled upon the waves of moonlit seas,

And pure as winds that never visit earth,

But spread the glowing fields, and build the domes

And towering pinnacles of upper air.

Born of the shade, and nourished where the peace

Of everlasting solitude abides,

It comes from inmost depths, where mighty trees

Throughout the lapse of silent centuries

Forever dream, and hear the silent voice

That sounds in nature's kindly ministrations,

And earthward-flowing harmonies of the stars.

The summit of yonder neighboring peak, that
    glowed

But now, as glows a sacrificial fire,

Against the vault of slowly darkening blue,

Has donned the sober garments of the night,

And looms, an awful shadow on the sky.

The varying shades that on that nearer height

Revealed the mighty, springing buttresses,

Like living things, with gorges sunk between,

Are all absorbed in one expanse of gray.

Between the summits slowly trailing clouds,

Like spotless messengers, bear secret words,

And sweet, mysterious greetings, each to each.

Slow, slow and gentle as soul-soothing Death,

Calm darkness gathers, bearing balmy sleep,

Boon of the East unto the weary West.

Nature, great-hearted mother, draws me close,

Whispers her consolations, from my heart

Drives all its petty worldliness, and breathes

Thereon a great, soul-satisfying peace.

All through the night, all through the solemn night,

Within whose bosom Nature hides her face,

The mountain top shall be my place of rest.

Perchance my spirit, cleansed and purified

By this aloofness from the world of men,

This nearness to the world of heaven's stars,

May somewhat from the silent voices learn,

And draw sweet comfort from the heart of night.

AN INVITATION.

Who will come with me and wander
Through the hills and valleys yonder?
   He whose torpid spirit never feels
   The touch of nature's manifold appeals,
Who never soars, but, well contented, crawls
Among these city walls,—
   Such a sluggard shall not be
   Fellow-traveller with me.

He whose heart rejoices
With all woodland voices,
   He who finds in zephyr strains
   Recompense for all his pains,
Who hath a lover's eye
For the colors of the sky,

And drinks the eager morning air
As a draught from worlds more fair,—
Such an one shall come, and be
Fellow-traveller with me.

Away, then ! away !
Who would brook delay
When the very air invites
To the ever new delights
That await us, where the daughter
Of the forest, Laughing Water,
Flings her liquid song upon the breeze,
Blends it with the music of the trees
In a symphony, whose measures
Sing of undiscovered treasures
For discerning eye and ear
Alone to see, alone to hear ?

Master Glossy-coat, the cricket,
From his little grassy thicket,

Chirps his message loud and shrill,

" Live with joy, and fear no ill."

Robins sing with lusty throats,

Launch abroad their joyful notes,

Whose tones of hearty cheer

Proclaim the hey-day of the year.

Hush ! Oh, hush !

'T is the tawny thrush

Pouring out his lay

To the ear of dying day

So divinely sweet and clear,

Heaven itself might joy to hear.

Sit beneath the trees and listen ;

You shall hear them all.

You shall see the waters glisten,

You shall see them fall

Down, down from the edge

Of the overhanging ledge

To the rock encircled pool,

Where they tarry, clear and cool,

Ere they dance away

Boisterous and gay,

Rushing swiftly, stealing slow,

To the meadow lands below.

Come, O come, my friend, and be

Fellow-traveller with me.

SPRING NIGHT.

Homeward I went from thee, beneath the light

Of spring-tide moon and stars, whose wondrous

    show

Of beauty o'er the firmament of night

Filled my glad heart to tearful overflow.

The zephyr-voice of nature breathed a song

Of praise more sweet than ever art of man

Could frame in words or music ; and along

The tender sky, an unsubstantial span

Of clouds as faint as fleecy foam of sea,

Lay like heaven's smile, above earth's shadowed

    face ;

And all things, filled with holy ecstasy,

Seemed to give thanks for this most heavenly grace.

I too gave thanks, that I this sight should see,

But more, for my heart's love, and thine for me.

THE PINE TREE.

Long ago, upon a mountain headland
Grew a pine tree. Far above its fellows
Raised the tree its host of spreading branches,
Held its green against the blue of heaven.
First to catch the light, as happy Morning
Laughed her glow along the low horizon ;
Last to lose the gleam, when dark-eyed Evening
Drew her veil, and sending forth her shadows,
Wooed the world to prove the sweets of slumber.

Through the night, the multitude of branches
Made an inner night of deeper blackness,
Where the owls, and things that love the darkness,
Came and sat long hours, and with the midnight

Held communion.   And by day the warblers,

Yellow-throated, hopped along the branches,

Or with sprightly, silent wing went flitting ;

And the burden of the song they uttered

Was the very soul of dreamy languor,

Suiting well the faint, mysterious music

Of the pine beneath the sultry noontide—

Blending with it as the zephyr mingles

With the far-off music of the ocean.

Through the changes of unnumbered seasons

Had the mountain held this lofty wood-king,

Springing heavenward like an aspiration.

And by day and night, while centuries vanished,

Winds had played with varying stress upon it,

From the light caresses of the zephyr,

To the wrenching fury of the tempest.

And the tree became a wondrous singer,

Strenuous, vibrant, true in all its fibres,

Harmonizing with the soul of nature.

Every tone of every song it uttered—

Whether loud, as roars the flood of waters

Rushing furious down the mountain gorges ;

Whether soft, as sighs the breath of noonday

Drifting dreamily above the forest—

Was the voice of root, and trunk, and branches,

Mingled all in one accordant heart-song.

From the vault-illuming constellations

In eternal march across the heavens,

Silent songs descended ; and the pine tree

Heard the chorus of their mingled voices

Pulsing through the palpitating ether,

Sweet and gentle as the soul of silence,

Large and gracious with a love eternal.

Hushed with awe the mighty monarch listened.

Then with reverent voice he breathed responses,

Sang a sacred soul-song to the star-world.

When the winds came raging, and the tempest
Stirred the pulse of night to wild commotion—
When the sky was luminous with lightning
And the hills were shaken with the thunder—
Then the pine tree revelled in the tumult,
As the warrior glories in the battle.
Oh! the sight was noble, when the monarch,
Singing to the ear of night his anthems,
Roaring back responses to the storm-king,
Was revealed by sheeted lightning, standing
As a lofty, pointed mass of blackness,
Tossing to and fro against the heavens
In the joy of elemental fury !

Ages since have flown ; and now the pine tree
Stands no more upon the mountain headland.
On the lofty place that knew and loved him
Countless trees have grown and died ; but never
One that held its head so high to heaven,

Never one that sang such glorious anthems,

Sang so sweetly to the jocund morning,

Chanted so divinely to the midnight.

TRANSFORMATION.

Only a hut, as mean, to thee,
  As any hovel in the land ;
A palace fair it is to me,
  For there I dared to kiss thy hand.

Ah, Sweet ! if that can work for me
  A change so wonderful as this,
The whole wide world a heaven will be,
  When I thy lovely lips may kiss.

A VISION OF POESY.

On the summits, where rosy-faced Morning en-
    counters black Night,
Where shadowy phantoms are routed before the
    new light,
The curtains of darkness were lifted, the world
    awoke fair on the sight.

O'er the eastern horizon the Day-God his banner
    unfurled,
Up the gorges like vanishing spirits the vapors
    were whirled,
Day's morning-smile brightened the heavens, and
    joy flew abroad o'er the world.

From the depths of the lightening valleys, from
    blossoming leas,

From the vault of encompassing heaven, from
    thundering seas,
She came to her place in her beauty, on the wings
    of the rapturous breeze.

Of the mists of the conquering Morning her gar-
    ments were made,
By winds interwoven and fashioned through sun-
    light and shade—
By tempests that ravage the ocean, by zephyrs that
    freshen the glade.

The breath of the dawn was within her, and deep
    in her eyes,
Transfigured to something diviner, the light of the
    skies
Shone lovely as lingering sunlight, on sea-reaches
    when the day dies.

Her presence was fresh with the odor of opening
    flowers,

Her glances were lit with the light of her heavenly
    powers,
And forth from her spirit came peace, and the
    balm of beneficent hours.

The song of the pines in the forest, the moan of
    the firs,
The sigh of the larch, that awakens and languidly
    stirs—
Their music was heard in her singing, their mys-
    tical meaning was hers.

And hers was the voice of the river that courses
    the plain,
The laugh of the stream in the woodland, the song
    of the rain,
The sweep and the rush of the waters that break
    with a roar on the main.

Her voice was the soul of all music that springs
    undefiled,

As pure as first whispers that waken the heart of a
child.

She spoke, and the earth paused to listen; she
sang, and the universe smiled.

THE MUSE DISDAINFUL.

Wandering in the woods one day,
I saw my gentle Muse at play.
   Here she floated, there she flew,
   This way turning, that way too,
Sported at her pleasure,
   High, and low, and every way,
   Shedding joy upon the day
In a rhythmic measure.

Hers was such a protean power,
Now she seemed a lovely flower ;
   Now she seemed to take
   The semblance of a stream, and wake
A joyance with her song,
Frolicking along

With a merry toss and tumble,
With melodious roar and rumble.

She was bright with morning dews,
She was gay with rainbow hues,
  And in her face, the might
  Of more than earthly light
Proclaimed her power,
And poured a glory into every hour.

"Come," I cried, "O thou most fair,
  To my heart.
Come, and chant thy music there,
  That a part
Of the rapture that is thine
I may drink, and make it mine;
  For my hungry spirit longs
  To taste the bliss of thy celestial songs."

Thus I sued her, thus I pleaded,

But my prayer was all unheeded.

  Here and there, round and round,

  Through the air, o'er the ground,

Now she tripped it, now she flew,

With a grace forever new.

  Howsoe'er I courted,

  She but laughed and sported,

Still pursued her joyful way,

Scorning e'en to say me nay.

Because my Muse disdained me so,

Shall I court Despair? ah, no;

  Rather let me keep good cheer,

  For again she will appear.

If my sense be tuned aright

To winds, and trees, and streams, and light,—

  If the voice of all sweet things that be

  Find an answering melody in me—

That shall be a blessed day ;

For the Maid will come to me, and stay

In my breast, until erelong

I may learn some measure of her song.

TO THE SEA.

Out of thy bosom forever, endlessly striving and
yearning,

Voicing the pulse of the world, rises thy song, O
Sea.

Over the globe, from the zone where voices of ice-
fettered mountains

Answer the roar of thy surge with echoing cry and
moan,

Unto the sun-warm sands that are glad with the kiss
of thy waters,

Ever thou lavest the earth, ever thy song flows free.

What do I hear in the thundering roar of thy boisterous billows?

What do I hear in the tone of thy wonderful chant,
O Sea?

Silent and reverent I wait, till forth from thy mystical measures
Sweetly emerges a voice, sounding an anthem of joy.
Under its spell I behold, in the tender effulgence of morning,
Fronting emblazoning forms that float on the face of young day,
Shores that resound with thy song, and rejoice in thy gentle caresses—
Sea-loving sands, attired as a bride in a garment of foam.
Fresh are the breezes, and sweet; for they come from the heart of mid-ocean,
Bearing a greeting of joy from the deep to the welcoming land.

Changed is thy song, O Sea. The beautiful shore is departed,
Gone are the glorious skies, vanished the wakening morn.

The breath of mid-ocean, that came as a zephyr in-
viting to slumber,

Rises, and rises, and swells to a frightful, demoniac
roar.

Hosts of encountering waves, in the fury of horrid
contention,

Leaping aloft, are caught in the hurricane's grasp,
and borne

Skyward, as mists that gather by night in the gorges
of mountains

Are carried on high by the blustering breath of awak-
ening day.

Ocean and cloud are as one, in a pillar of murky
destruction,

Whose tortuous path is strewn with ghostly, inani-
mate forms.

Mariners' shrieks of despair are drowned in the
deafening tumult,

Wild supplications are lost in the pitiless thunder of
doom.

Thou fertile purveyor to Death, thy mighty embrace
doth encompass

The whole broad lands of the earth, and thou liest
in wait for thy prey

As a merciless monster, whose arms are strong with
a strength elemental,

Whose jaws are insatiate, whose breast is a vast, un-
satisfied grave.

Changed is thy song, O Sea. Thou art clothed with
the shadows of midnight,

The voice of thy billows is hushed, thy wandering
waves are at rest.

Above thee, innumerous stars swing round in majestic procession,

And through the vast reaches of space thou hearest
the sound of their song.

Thou receivest the spirit of Night, and she speaks a
    dread word to thy waters,

That spreads from the heart of thy realms to the
    bounds of thy farthermost shores.

The voice is unheard of man ; but its accents are
    awful as thunder

To the soul of thy fathomless wastes ; and unto the
    legions of stars,

And the vault of encompassing night, and the world
    of enveloping darkness,

Thou whisperest out of thy deeps, thou singest an
    answering song.

O Sea, to my spiritless ear thou art striving and
    yearning to utter

The wordless message the stars, and the measure-
    less realms of night

Sang low to thy listening waves. But alas ! as a
    vanishing echo

It hovers beyond my ken, and mocks the despair of
my heart.

For the veil of the flesh is strong that wraps and en-
cumbers the spirit,

And I hearken and wait in vain for the word thou
art singing to me.

www.ingramcontent.com/pod-product-compliance
Lightning Source LLC
Chambersburg PA
CBHW030551270326
41927CB00008B/1598